MY CREATION

NITIN

ARVIND SHARMA

Copyright © Arvind Sharma
All Rights Reserved.

This book has been published with all efforts taken to make the material error-free after the consent of the author. However, the author and the publisher do not assume and hereby disclaim any liability to any party for any loss, damage, or disruption caused by errors or omissions, whether such errors or omissions result from negligence, accident, or any other cause.

While every effort has been made to avoid any mistake or omission, this publication is being sold on the condition and understanding that neither the author nor the publishers or printers would be liable in any manner to any person by reason of any mistake or omission in this publication or for any action taken or omitted to be taken or advice rendered or accepted on the basis of this work. For any defect in printing or binding the publishers will be liable only to replace the defective copy by another copy of this work then available.

This book is dedicated to my family

Contents

Foreword vii

Acknowledgements ix

1. Pics 1
2. My Creation 12
3. Some New 20
4. Old Creation 27
5. Wow Great Pics 34
6. Amazing Pic 39
7. Great 43
8. Complete Year Pic 46

Foreword

I am dedicating this book to my bro who has always been my best friend , biggest support and whose never-say-die spirit and moral values have made me what I am today.

I am grateful to God for blessing me with such a loving and caring family.

Acknowledgements

To accomplishment, however big or small, is possible without the support of one's friends and the Almighty, book may have been authored by me, but could not have been possible without the support of many people.

My friends and family have always been special to me, always encouraging me to chase my dreams. My father and brother have been the biggest inspirations in my life.

Thanks to all my friends, fans, readers and critics for showering me with so much love and affection for my third book. My Beloved's IIT Plans. Each review and email that came to me mattered. Frankly, I had never thought I would pen down another one, but your support and encouragement made it happen. I look forward to hearing from all of you again.

Special thanks to the families and friends of people who have been covered in the book for opening their hearts and sharing their lives good and bad moments with me.

And finally, each time I was stuck with my words or faced any kind of dilemma, my faith and belief in God helped me go the extra mile. Thank you, God.

CHAPTER ONE

pics

MY CREATION

Nitesh and his sister himani

bhavana

MY CREATION

· 4 ·

ARVIND SHARMA

MY CREATION

ARVIND SHARMA

MY CREATION

ARVIND SHARMA

MY CREATION

CHAPTER TWO

my creation

MY CREATION

MY CREATION

CHAPTER THREE

some new

MY CREATION

angry man ?

MY CREATION

CHAPTER FOUR

old creation

MY CREATION

MY CREATION

CHAPTER FIVE

wow great pics

MY CREATION

CHAPTER SIX

amazing pic

MY CREATION

ARVIND SHARMA

MY CREATION

CHAPTER SEVEN

great

MY CREATION

ARVIND SHARMA

CHAPTER EIGHT

complete year pic

nitesh and his bro

www.ingramcontent.com/pod-product-compliance
Lightning Source LLC
LaVergne TN
LVHW021738060526
838200LV00052B/3341